The Ghosts of Williamsburg

...And Nearby Environs

by L. B. Taylor, Jr.

Hauntingly yours,

16th Printing
1996

Photographs by the Author
Illustrations by Isobel Pettengell

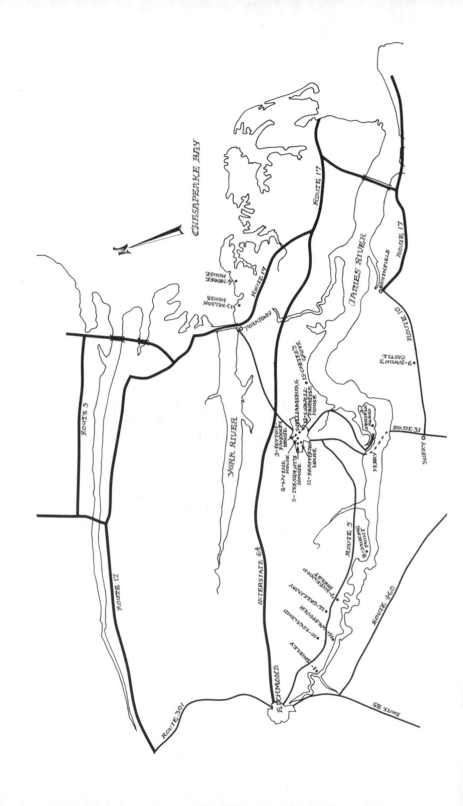

CONTENTS

Introduction

Perhaps it is apropos that hidden away in an area so richly endowed and meticulously documented in early American tradition are the secret legends and colorful folklore of ghosts and haunted houses. They abound in Colonial Williamsburg, along the corners of the historic triangle in Jamestown and Yorktown, across the James River in Surry County, and all along "plantation row" off route 5 which connects Williamsburg with Richmond.

These strange tales of brooding spirits will not be found in the scholarly and thoroughly researched journals which record the events and times of the Virginia Colony from the day the first settlers landed in 1607. Nor are they related in the normal discourses espoused by tour guides. How do you explain and authenticate a ghost? Yet the stories, like the houses in which they originated, have persisted down through the centuries.

And, in their own way, many of them are documented. For these ghosts have been seen, heard or had their presences felt by some highly credible witnesses whose integrity and sincerity are beyond reproach. Consider that among those who have experienced some form of mysterious psychic phenomena are Dr. Thomas Graves, President of the College of William and Mary, and his predecessor, Dr. Davis Paschall; Harrison Tyler, owner of Sherwood Forest and the grandson of U.S. President John Tyler; and Wilford Kale, the respected Williamsburg bureau chief of the Richmond Times Dispatch.

Skeptics may contend that such occurrences as the appearance of wispy apparitions, the late-night sounds of muffled footsteps or of moans and cries, or the playing of mischievious pranks by invisible sources all are happenings that can be explained by rational means. But can they? And are not such arguments locked within the present and limited boundaries of human understanding? Who can say for sure whether or not there is a psychic world that still lurks in the dark recesses of the unknown, the key to which may lie somewhere in the future?

In writing this manuscript, the author does not deem to

make a statement for or against the existence of ghosts. The sole purpose of this book is to entertain, by collecting and recording an interesting assortment of tales that have been passed along by generations of Virginians.

Are the spirits described herein real? That, dear reader, you must decide for yourself. Enjoy.

Shirley Plantation

1. The Strange Saga of Aunt Pratt

It is, unquestionably, one of the most magnificent original colonial mansions in the United States. Architectural historians believe that parts of its impressive design were inspired by the second governor's palace at Williamsburg.

The site upon which the great house sits is steeped in early Virginia history and tradition. It was, in fact, founded in 1613 — just six years after the first settlers landed at nearby Jamestown, and a full seven years *before* the Pilgrims arrived at Plymouth Rock.

This is Shirley Plantation, located at a point overlooking a scenic bend in the James River about halfway between Williamsburg and Richmond.

It was originally owned by Sir Thomas West, the first Royal Governor of the Colony of Virginia. He named it in honor of his wife's father, Sir Thomas Sherley of Whiston, England. Later, the plantation gained eminence as the home of Colonel Edward Hill, who held many high offices in the colony through the mid-17th century, including speaker of the Assembly of Burgesses and treasurer of Virginia. The estate has been in the Hill and Carter families for more than 300 years.

The present house was begun in 1723 by the third Edward Hill, also a man of status in the colony. He built it for his daughter, Elizabeth, who married John Carter, son of the legendary King Carter. It took nearly 50 years to complete the construction and was done as one author described it, "with a lavish disregard for cost seldom displayed in the building of even great mansions."

This handsome brick house stands three stories tall with rows of dormer windows projecting from the roof on all sides. It has huge twin chimneys which flank a large carved pineapple, the colonial symbol for hospitality. Two splendid, two-story porticos, each with four white pillars, set off the front of the building with stylish grace.

Inside, 18th century artisans fashioned superb panelling and delicate carvings. A major design feature is an elegant carved walnut staircase which rises for three stories without visible support — the only one of its kind in America. The entire house is filled with exquisite furnishings, crested silver, and interesting memorabilia assembled from the nine generations of the families which have lived there.

Shirley was a well-known center of hospitality 100 years before and during the American Revolution. George Washington and Thomas Jefferson were guests there as were numerous other prominent Virginians. There are also many interesting anecdotes and stories about events which have transpired at Shirley.

One of the more charming concerns the time a young and beautiful Anne Hill Carter was carrying a punchbowl across the dining room when it began slipping from her fingers. She was rescued by a dashing young military officer — "Light Horse" Harry Lee. Not long afterwards they were married at Shirley. Their son became one of the most famous of all Virginians — and Americans. He was Robert E. Lee.

Another colorful tale had its origins during the Civil War when Federal troops occupied Charles City County. One of the young Carter men who lived at Shirley then was serving with the Confederate Army when he learned that his mother was gravely ill at home. Using knowledge of the local terrain he had learned as a boy, he made his way through Union lines surrounding the area and sneaked into the house to visit his mother, only to be betrayed by an unfaithful servant.

A Union officer and several of his men were dispatched to search the mansion. They found nothing, and were about to abandon their quest when the officer spotted an entry to the attic behind a concealing bookcase. In the attic the young Carter hid in back of chimney stacks and apparently eluded the officer, for he returned to his men saying there was no one in the attic. Carter waited until dark and then rejoined his troops.

It was not until decades later that a relative of that officer, during a visit to Shirley, told tour hostesses that young Carter actually had been seen in the attic, but the officer's "conscience overcame his compulsion to duty."

Perhaps the most compelling legend of Shirley revolves around the ghost of a former resident and family member. For

Shirley, like a number of its neighboring plantations along the James, is haunted.

This is the fascinating, and, to this day, the inexplicable story of "Aunt Pratt," or more specifically, of her famous portrait. She was reportedly a sister of Edward Hill, and was born late in the 17th century. Little is known of her, but it is said there always was a certain air of mystery about the woman.

Whatever, one of the things for which Shirley is noted is its fine collection of family portraits. Apparently, Aunt Pratt's portrait occupied a suitable place in a downstairs bedroom for a number of years after her death. Then, as a new generation of the family took over occupancy and decided to redecorate, the portrait was taken down and banished to the obscurity of the attic.

Aunt Pratt, or, if you will, her spirit, did not take kindly to this. In fact, she made what family members described as a "mighty disturbance." This usually took the form of the sound of a woman rocking in the attic late at night. A number of guests, as well as Hills and Carters told of hearing the incessant rocking on certain nights. Yet when they summoned courage to check the attic, all was still and quiet. Nothing was amiss, although they admitted getting chills up their spines when they looked into the eyes of Aunt Pratt's portrait amidst the dust, cobwebs and clutter of the attic.

Eventually, the restlessness of her spirit proved too much for the occupants of the house. Prudently, they chose to bring the portrait back down and hang it in its rightful place. Once this was done, the strange rocking sounds were never heard again.

Intriguingly, however, this did not end the troubled travels of Aunt Pratt. A few years ago the Virginia Travel Council scoured about the Commonwealth in search of relics, antiques, and other items associated with psychic phenomena for a tourist promotion they were assembling in New York City. Council officials, having heard the story of Aunt Pratt's ghostly rocking, asked if they might borrow her portrait for the exhibit. And so, "she" was crated and shipped north. But no sooner had she been hung on a wall when she once again "came to life," openly venting her displeasures at being so far away from home.

According to credible accounts, the portrait was once observed "swinging" in its display case. Then one morning workmen found the portrait lying on the floor several feet away from the case, and, in their words, "heading toward the exit."

As a security measure, officials had Aunt Pratt locked up in a closet when not on exhibit. One night a maintenance crew became unnerved when they heard "knocking and crying" coming from the locked closet. No one was inside. The next morning the portrait mysteriously had escaped from the closet and was lying on the floor outside.

At this point a psychic expert was called in. She studied the portrait carefully and felt strong sensations. The psychic believed there were two women involved in the portrait, and two theories were offered in possible explanation. One contended that there are actually two portraits, one painted on top of the other. The supposition here is that the original lady involved has, perhaps for centuries, been struggling to regain her identity and respect. The other consideration is that a model perhaps sat in for Aunt Pratt during the original painting, again pointing to the conceivability of a deep-rooted identity crisis.

Whether or not either of these ideas has any validity, the psychic expert was convinced that there was indeed a powerful spiritual phenomenon associated with the portrait; that the person involved was somehow trying to convey her irritance at being, to her mind, indignantly displayed.

Many experts agree that spirits which manifest themselves in the manner Aunt Pratt did, are actually ghosts of residences who believe, even though they are dead and gone, that the house they lived in still belongs to them. This seems the most plausible explanation in Aunt Pratt's instance.

Subsequent events added credence to this line of thought. On its way back south from the New York showing, the portrait was taken to a shop in Richmond so repairs could be made on the now battered frame. When it was picked up, the shop owner said that ever since Aunt Pratt had been in his care, he heard bells ringing. This, he deemed at best odd, and at worst, eerily haunting, because, he added, there were no bells of any kind in his shop.

The portrait was then restored once more to its proper place on a wall in the downstairs bedroom. Since that time, there have been no further strange occurrences at Shirley.

Aunt Pratt, at last, was home.

"Aunt Pratt"

2. The Curse Tree of Jamestown Island

It would be highly unlikely that you would find the story in any of the countless history books which chronicle the life and times of the settlers at Jamestown and the colonists at Williamsburg. Nor would you be apt to hear tour guides relate this strange tale if you visit the major attractions at Jamestown Festival Park or Colonial Williamsburg.

Rather, you must travel somewhat off the beaten track, to Jamestown Island itself, about a mile or so away from the Park. This is the actual site, where, in May 1607, the first American settlers landed. The area today is maintained jointly by the Association for the Preservation of Virginia Antiquities and the National Park Service.

Just beyond Jamestown Memorial Church, which was built in 1907 upon the foundation of an original church erected in 1617, lies a small, quiet, tree-shaded cemetary containing only a handful of graves. It is here that James and Sarah Harrison Blair are buried.

Chances are, unless you are more than a casual buff of colonial history, the name of James Blair is unfamiliar. This is an unfortunate injustice to the man, for he was an important figure in Virginia's history during the latter days of the 17th century and well into the 18th century. Born in Scotland and educated at the University of Edinburgh, he filled, according to the markings on his tombstone, "the offices of preacher of the gospel for 54 years."

He also served as a faithful "councillor" to the British Governor and subsequently as a Governor of the Colony. Further, he has been described by biographers as a "very powerful man," and as the "chief force" behind the founding of the College of William and Mary, the second oldest institution of higher learning in the country.

On a more personal note, his tombstone points out that "the comliness (sic) of a handsome face adorned him...he entertained elegantly in a cheerful, hospitable manner without luxury...in affability, he excelled." And it is in the combination of these attractive features that this tale had its origins.

It was in the year 1687. Sarah Harrison, by popular accounts, was then a strikingly beautiful young lady of 17, who, because of the relatively comfortable financial position of her parents, was an active participant in the plantation-circle social life along the lower James River. The oldest daughter of the "mighty" Colonel Benjamin Harrison of Wakefield Plantation, a wealthy land owner, she has been variously described as vivacious, full of life, and head strong. Some intimate that she was a forerunner to the late 20th century women's liberation movement because it is alleged she spoke her piece whenever she felt slighted by the young men of the day.

Despite this strongly independent nature — or perhaps because of it — in conjunction with her natural beauty, Sarah Harrison was actively wooed by a number of handsome and eligible suitors. It was in 1687, according to Sam Robinson, a long time caretaker at Jamestown Island, that "she firs' sign a (marriage) contract with a young gennelman by name of William Roscoe. He was 22 and she was in her 17." The contract, Robinson said, stated that "she would never marry to any man on earth (other than Roscoe) as long as he was alive, so hep her God, signed Sarah Harrison."

However, three weeks later she met the handsome, charismatic Blair. She was swept off her feet. Her parents were not so enchanted. There were two immediate problems. She already was engaged to a perfectly acceptable (to them) young man. Secondly, James Blair at the time was 31 years old, nearly twice Sarah's age. As Robinson colorfully phrased it, "in olden day iffen young girl was to marry elder gennelman (it) was called a disgrace to her parents. 'Course now day an' time it (doesn't) make any diffen (difference) how old dey is jes as dey has de money."

What immediately ensued was the expected; a bitter rift between daughter and parents. This intensified when Sarah broke her initial engagement and told them she planned to marry the Reverend Blair. Through reasoning, arguments and threats, her parents tried everything to discourage the union, but Sarah's mind was made up.

As Robinson recounted the story: "She break the contract

then with her lover William Roscoe, causin' his death made of hearbreakin' and marry to Dr. Blair." It is not known if her parents even attended the affair. One version, though, has it that Sarah refused to utter the words "to obey" at the ceremony. As it was said, she had a mind of her own, this girl.

Her parents would not give up even after the wedding. They sought to have the marriage annulled. But here, fate took a curious hand. One day while on an outing in their carriage with Sarah's kid sister they were caught in a fierce thunderstorm. In Robinson's words: ". . . Colonel Benjamin, Mrs. Hannah his wife, and his baby daughter — all three of them was kill up on Route 5 up at Berkeley by lightning. . . so they didn't get a chance in life to separate Miss Sarah from Dr. Blair."

Sarah and James Blair, it is said, lived a happy life together as man and wife. She died in 1713 at the age of 42 still unforgiven by her family. Says Robinson: "By disobeying her parents in life and marry to Dr. Blair again' her family consent, the Harrison family. . . buried her away from her family" On her tombstone are the Latin words which, translated, say, "In sacred memory, here lies in the hope of blessed resurrection the body of Mrs. Sarah Blair. . . exceedingly beloved and lamented."

Her husband lived on for 30 years, contributing significantly to the continued growth and prosperity of the young colony. When he died in 1743, he was laid to rest at a site "six inches beyond on the left hand side" of his wife's grave.

In the year 1750, seven years after Blair's death, fate intervened again. Robinson told what happened this way: "Was a stoned in fence around the two graves six inches apart side by side." A sycamore tree "came up between 'em as a little wild sapling. Wasn't anythin' deed (did) to prevent de tree or protect de grave so as it growed it caught in the center tomb there by Dr. Blair, break the stones then in two both ends, right where her stone were joined to Dr. Blair stone, push her tomb up out de groun' above Dr. Blair and push de back on the head end seven feet from her husband back over to de right within six inches of her (third) elder sister, Mother,

Father and younger sister...and leave Dr. Blair on de left hand side in a stone by himself."

And so, as the legend went, Sarah's parents, who could not dissolve her marriage with Blair while they were alive, were finally able to separate the lovers after death. The late Robert L. Ripley wrote about this odd incident in his "Believe it or not" column, calling the sycamore the "mother-in-law tree." Others have referred to it as the "curse tree." Robinson, who told the story many times, once to Queen Elizabeth of England during her visit to Jamestown Island in 1957 upon the 350th anniversary of the first settlers' landing, said: "the mother-in-law didn' get a chance in life to separate her daughter Sarah from Dr. Blair, but...she did come back and plant the old sycamore to separate her."

There is a bizarre footnote to the story. Several years ago the old sycamore tree, which had grown to considerable size, died and was cut out of the site, although the broken bricks

Curse Tree at Jamestown Island

15

and cracked tombs were left as they were, pushed apart.

Soonafter, a new sycamore sapling sprang up in the exact same spot where the original tree had stood, and flourishes today. It is, some say, the strong will of Sarah's parents reasserting itself from beyond the graves. The legend lives on.

3. The Nagging Shrew of Peyton Randolph House

It is one of the showpiece houses of Colonial Williamsburg. Nestled on a scenic corner amidst towering oak trees, Peyton Randolph House draws hundreds of tourists every week. None of them are aware, however, that it is haunted; that in a mysterious oak-paneled second floor bedroom the spectre of a deeply disturbed woman who possibly lived there 150 to 200 years ago periodically reappears, apparently to warn guests of impending tragedy.

Few people know of this phenomenon, and fewer still will talk about it. Employees who guide visitors through the house daily, and workers who maintain the residence are reluctant to discuss the issue.

Some won't talk out of fear; others are afraid they will be called fools if they told what they have seen and heard when no one else was around. But of those who know the house well, none doubt that there is something inexplicably strange about it. Too many people have experienced similar eerie phenomena within its historic walls for more than a century and a half. Too many people have seen or heard the old woman who periodically haunts it.

The last person known to have seen her was Mrs. Helen Hall Mason, a retired school mistress of redoubtable character. In Williamsburg in October 1962 for the wedding of a close family friend, Mrs. Mason stayed at the house as a guest of its owner. She slept in the oak paneled room. The room itself is small and is located in the back end of the house. It is paneled floor-to-ceiling in red oak, which is unusual architecturally for the early 18th century, when it was built. Such paneling then was considered the heighth of luxury and restrained elegance. There is a fireplace in a corner of the room and there are two narrow windows, typical of that era, facing north. The room has a high ceiling. A small low-post bed lies next to one of the windows, resting on the heart pine floor.

On that particular night in 1962, sometime after midnight, Mrs. Mason was awakened from a deep sleep with the sensation that someone was calling or summoning her. She sat up and was startled at the sight of a woman standing at the foot of her bed. At first, she thought it was her hostess, but then as her eyes adjusted to the darkness she could see that it was not.

It was an old woman dressed in a long flowing gown and a peignoir typical of the nightwear of 18th century women of means. Atop her head was a cap. Mrs. Mason could barely make out any details, but she did clearly observe that the woman obviously was distraught and agitated and stood there nervously wringing her hands.

Mrs. Mason sat up straighter and asked the woman what she wanted. There was no reply. Then Mrs. Mason saw something that made her gasp. She could scarcely catch her breath. The bright moonlight streaming into the room through a window shone through the woman: She was transparent. She was not a real person, rather a mystic, shadowy figure of a woman. Within a few minutes the wispy apparition disappeared.

The next morning Mrs. Mason related the story to her

Peyton Randolph House

friends. She told them she had not been afraid of the woman, but that she had the strong feeling that whoever, or whatever, it was she saw had come to give her a message of some kind. And she believed that the message was to warn her of impending tragedy.

Mrs. Mason had never been in the room before. She thought her friends might laugh at her for such a crazy tale, but they did not. In fact, they were not even surprised. Over the years they had heard the same experience repeated in precise detail several times before by others. The story of the woman with wringing hands has been told in Williamsburg for more than 150 years. But Mrs. Mason, like others before her who saw the woman, was not aware of the legend when she slept in the room.

Who is this mysterious woman, and why does she appear at certain times, always in the same place? What awful story of anguish and despair does she conceal? What are the hidden secrets of Peyton Randolph House?

No one knows the exact answers to these questions, but through research, investigation and speculation there are some clues. The house was built sometime around 1715, during the heyday of Williamsburg as the capital of Colonial Virginia. Its first owner, Sir John Randolph was, in his day, the most distinguished lawyer in Virginia. He served as clerk of the House of Burgesses in 1728 and later became the only colonial Virginian to be knighted by the King of England.

Sir John died in 1737 and willed the house to his wife for her lifetime, and after that to his second son, Peyton, for whom the house later was named. Peyton was born about 1721, and became one of the leading statesmen of Colonial America. He served as speaker of the House of Burgesses for nine years, and was chosen president of the first Continental Congress in Philadelphia in 1774.

He died a year later. His wife, Mrs. Betty Harrison Randolph continued to live in the house for some years afterward, and it was occupied by Count de Rochambeau as a temporary headquarters in 1781 just before the Yorktown campaign which ended the Revolutionary War. It also is known that General George Washington and Lafayette dined there shortly after the war's end. The house later was sold out of the Randolph family, and in 1824, the owner, Mrs. Mary Monroe Peachy, served as hostess to General Lafayette during his visit to the United States.

The history of the house for the next century and a half is more difficult to follow. The Virginia capital was moved to Richmond in 1780, and Williamsburg became a quiet and all but forgotten town. The house passed through a number of different owners, and it slowly gained notoriety as a residence of sadness and tragedy. Many people met strange and untimely deaths there during the 19th and early 20th centuries.

One of the Peachy children, for example, fell from a tree in the yard and was killed. Several other children died in the house. There have been at least two and maybe more suicides there. It is hard to determine exactly how many because in earlier times families did not report deaths as suicides. It is known that one gentleman shot himself in front of the fireplace in the drawing room. Two brothers are reported to have gotten into a violent struggle in the oak paneled room, leading to lasting bitterness and suffering.

Then, shortly after the end of the Civil War, a brilliant young scholar, who had joined the Confederate Army when he was only 14 years old, moved into the house. He had lost his family in the war, and one of the Peachy family members took him in as a boarder. He lived on the second floor next to the oak paneled room, and attended the College of William and Mary.

Soonafter, he developed a severe case of tuberculosis and died a painful, agonizing death in the house. For years afterward there was an overwhelming sense of sadness and grief which lingered, as one servant described it, "to the point of oppressiveness."

It was as if the house was jinxed. Superstitious servants would not speak of the many tragedies. Nor would they talk of the weird happenings that occurred. Occasionally at night someone would be heard walking across the wooden floors upstairs in heavy boots with spurs. But when the rooms were searched no one could be found. At other times there would be loud crashes of glass, such as a large mirror smashing to the

Illustration by Caryl Moore

floor. But again, investigations would find no one or nothing amiss. Many people experienced both these occurrences at various times through the years.

More recently, a Colonial Williamsburg tour hostess reported seeing a man dressed in colonial costume sitting in a chair in a downstairs room. He vanished before her eyes. Another woman who experienced a psychic occurrence in the house is a former tour hostess now retired. She won't talk about her harrowing encounter today, but she did confide her story to a few friends.

Once, when she was in the house alone, before it was opened for visitations one day, she was standing at the top of the staircase on the second floor, adjacent to the oak paneled bedroom. Suddenly, she felt the strong sensation of an "evil spirit" trying to push her down the stairs. It was a frightening experience, which passed in a few minutes, but she will never forget it.

And then there is the mystery woman, who always stands at the foot of the guest bed in the oak-paneled room. She has been seen by numerous visitors who have slept in the room, always under the same circumstances as Mrs. Mason. All persons who have seen her have said they were awakened from a deep sleep, and they felt the woman was there to warn them of some danger. One visitor and his wife were so alarmed they reportedly fled from the house in the middle of the night dressed only in their pajamas.

Who is this woman and what is she trying to tell? Is she a past resident of the house who has seen the generations of suffering and grief? Is she afraid the house will foster yet more sadness and tragedy on unsuspecting visitors? Is she trying to say most of the violence and death occurred in or near the oak-paneled room?

Many people think so, although no one knows for sure. But those who have seen or experienced the odd phenomena which manifests in the Peyton Randolph House cannot be shaken from their belief that the woman and the bootsteps and the crashing glass all are real and not imagined. They have all told the same story down to the last detail. They have all heard the same mysterious sounds and seen the woman dressed in the same night clothes.

Could the fact that so many people have shared the identical experience at different times over a century and a half be a coincidence? This seems highly unlikely. Yet to this day no one has been able to explain the strange sounds and the sightings in Peyton Randolph House, although many experts have tried.

And so, as the tourists continue to file through the house, tour guides speak of the many accomplishments of Peyton Randolph; of the architectural features of the colonial era; and of the times Washington dined there and Lafayette slept there. But no mention is ever made of the tragedies and suffering which have plagued the house, or of the woman who periodically haunts the oak-paneled room on the second floor.

4. History Haunts Moore House

History comes alive in more ways than one at the Moore House set amidst the Yorktown battlefield. It was in this wooden frame structure that on the afternoon of October 18, 1781, representatives of General George Washington and Lord Cornwallis met to negotiate terms of the British surrender to the American forces, in effect ending the Revolutionary War.

Today, visitors to the reconstructed Moore House are greeted by a National Park Service employee dressed as a French soldier of late 18th century vintage, complete with a French accent, who recomposes the historic setting that took place here more than two centuries ago. His presence adds a touch of color and realism to the scene.

Not part of the tour, however, is the alleged periodic presence of a ghost who occasionally has sent shivers up the

Moore House

spines of custodians and Park Service employees alike. "It is really eerie," one ranger has said. "Some of our people don't even like to talk about it."

Both the Moore House and the land upon which it sits have rich backgrounds. Barely 20 years after the founding of Jamestown in 1607, colonists began to settle along the shores of the York River. One of the first to acquire land here was a governor of Virginia, Sir John Harvey, who held 752 acres known as "York Plantation," on which Moore House now stands.

Harvey got in conflict with his fellow colonists and eventually suffered the indignity of having the mortgage on his property foreclosed. The land passed through several hands, and was acquired late in the 17th century by Major Lawrence Smith. He was a lawyer, commander of a fort in 1675 on the Indian frontier near Fredericksburg, a commander of loyalist forces during Bacon's Rebellion in 1676, and later a surveyor of Yorktown.

When he died in 1700 his large estate went to his second son, the younger Lawrence Smith. He is believed to have built Moore House in the early 1700s. After his death in 1739, the house and grounds passed to Augustine Moore, who had married Lawrence's daughter, Lucy Smith. In 1768 Moore purchased 500 acres of the old Smith estate together with the house. Sometime between 1768 and 1777, Augustine and Lucy Moore took up residence and continued to live here until their deaths in 1788 and 1797 respectively.

Moore descended from the Moore family of Elizabeth City County — a lineage which possibly began with John Moore who came to Virginia in 1620. Moore struck up a partnership with Thomas Nelson of Yorktown in a merchant career that proved to be "long and profitable."

When he died, he left his wife his household goods and "use of the estate until her death," and he willed the house to Nelson. By 1821 the property passed from the Nelson family and changed hands many times over the years.

If a house could talk, this one would have many stories to relate. Not only was it directly in the line of fire between American and British forces during the Revolutionary War, but it also stood between Union soldiers on Wormly Creek and Confederate troops in Yorktown during the Civil War. It was riddled with shell fire from the War between the States. Worse, foraging soldiers stripped away siding and other usable wood to keep warm during the chilly winter months. What was left of the house stood derelict until 1881 when much-needed repairs were made for the Centennial Celebration of the victory over Cornwallis. Efforts at that time to preserve it as a national landmark failed. Half a century later the Park Service restored Moore House to its original colonial appearance and it was formally dedicated on October 18-19, 1934.

What is not part of the official history of the house is the legend of the ghost who, some believe, remains there to this day, "to keep an eye on things." It is thought to be the spirit of Augustine Moore, Jr. Little is known of him.

One man who has researched the psychic phenomena associated with the house is Dave Jordan, an instructor of engineering at the Yorktown Coast Guard Reserve Training Center. He thinks young Moore was struck by a stray musket ball during the Revolutionary War fighting while he worked in the field. Jordan surmises, from what he has been able to piece together, that the lad, then less than 20 years old, staggered into the house and lay mortally ill for several days before he expired.

The stories of his spiritual return to his ancestral home, however, did not surface until after the Park Service restored the house. It was then that employees began to notice strange phenomena. They did not directly see, hear or feel the Moore lad's presence. It was more subtle than that.

"The maintenance people generally came into the house at seven in the morning to clean it up," says Park Service employee Christine Stoudt. "Sometimes they would change the sheets on the bed in the master bedroom upstairs. The covers would be left clean and straightened.

"Then, curiously, when the tour guides came in to begin their day three hours later, they would notice a deep impression on the bed covers, as if someone had laid down there. To the best of our knowledge no one had, because this room is roped off and no one is allowed inside. You view it from the hallway."

This has happened, Stoudt noted, on numerous occasions, and each time it caused a strong feeling of uneasiness among the custodians and the guides. No explanation for the phenomena has ever been offered. Stoudt also said that it has appeared, "any number of times," that someone has sat in a red velvet chair in the downstairs room where the Revolutionary War peace negotiations took place. Again, no one knows the cause.

In 1982 a psychic expert visited the house and said he definitely "felt a presence" in the upstairs bedroom. He said he experienced the vision of a man looking out the window. Dave Jordan, who studies psychic phenomena as a hobby, plans to photograph the bedroom using infra red film. This, he explains, would show "energy fields."

Meanwhile, the mystery of the rumpled bed and depressed seat cushion remains unsolved. Some who are familiar with the legend speculate that it is indeed the spirit of Augustine Moore, Jr., who died an agonizing death in the house so many years ago, and has returned to see that his home, so badly damaged through two historic wars, is, at last, safe and properly cared for.

5. The French Ghost of President's House

The house has withstood the ravages of time, fires, wars, a tornado, and occupation by foreign troops in its 250-plus year history. Yet today it remains an architectural showpiece of subtle elegance. It also is a residence of unsolved mysteries, for hidden within its walls are dark secrets of: a strange closet door that wouldn't stay shut; a skeleton embedded in brick; an enigmatic expression inscribed in an upstairs bedroom window; and the occasional wanderings of a restless military ghost.

The President's House at the College of William and Mary has been described by architectural historians as "the perfect Georgian" structure. Built in the familiar Queen Ann style, it features a steep roof, distinct vertical lines and impressively tall chimneys. The large, three-story brick building was designed by Henry Clay Jr., of Warwick County, who also completed the design for the Governor's Palace in Colonial Williamsburg as well as other college edifices.

The foundation was laid in July 1732, the same year George Washington was born. He later would be a guest in the house. Experts say this is one of only three original 18th century buildings in Williamsburg still used for the same purposes they were over 200 years ago. It has served all 24 William and Mary presidents and their families, ever since the college's first president, James Blair, moved into it in October 1733.

Through the centuries, the President's House has been noted as a symbol of hospitality for the entertaining of students and distinguished guests alike. In addition to Washington, U.S. presidents Thomas Jefferson, James Madison, John Tyler and everyone from Warren Harding through Dwight Eisenhower have been entertained there, many after receiving honorary degrees from the college.

"I just love this place," says Zoe Graves, wife of Tom Graves, current president of William and Mary. "Just think, Ben Franklin and Patrick Henry were here, and all the presidents. I believe they all left a certain spirit in the house. No house is devoid of spirits once the people have been here.

Quality of thoughts do remain. I feel we're companions to our predecessors who lived here, and to their guests. If only a house could talk. Think of the conversations that must have taken place here."

One famous guest who came uninvited, and, in fact, commandeered the house for a time was Lord Cornwallis, who set up temporary headquarters for his British troops here in 1781. In doing so, he evicted the Reverend James Madison, then president of the college and cousin of the future American president of the same name.

Shortly after Cornwallis abruptly vacated the house, during the final weeks of the Revolutionary War, it was used as a hospital for Lafayette's soldiers. In December 1781, a raging fire swept through the building. The wounded men escaped the flames, but much of the interior and its furnishings was ruined or damaged, although the two-foot-thick walls survived. The King of France then authorized funds for the building's renovation, which took nearly four years to complete.

But what of the unanswered mysteries of the house? The closet door in an upstairs bedroom, Mrs. Graves points out, is something that previous residents all had problems with. The door, it seems, would not stay shut.

"I've heard that people would close it only to have it pop right open," she says. "No one could find a reason why this happened."

Then one day many years ago a crew of workmen were making repairs in the house. While working in some crawl space above the ceiling on the third floor, they made a startling discovery. There, "pressed" into a brick wall, was a human skeleton. The bones were painstakingly removed, and ever since they were taken from the house, the closet door has shut without trouble.

"It certainly raises a lot of questions," Mrs. Graves says. "I've often wondered whose skeleton that was, and why was it pressed into the brick? How did it get there? Was it some form of inhumane torture? Curious."

Another fascinating question concerns the inscription on a window in a rear bedroom on the second floor. It says, cryptically, "Oh Fatal Day." Dr. Davis Paschall, former presi-

President's House

dent of the college, says he thinks it may have been done with a diamond ring, and may refer to a marriage date of one of the Tyler girls who wed a Dr. Wilson, associated with William and Mary early in the 20th century. Whatever the message meant, or whether it had pleasant or unpleasant connotations, has been lost in the storied lore of the house.

And then there is the ghost. "He's supposed to be the spirit of a French soldier who died of his wounds in the house," Mrs. Graves says. "He died in a small back room on the third floor, and the story is he still lingers between the second and third floors. I used to tell about him to young school children who came to the house. They would scream and shout, but I told them if they felt something grab them from their shoulders down, it was just 'him' giving them a love hug."

The legend is the soldier's footsteps can be heard descending the stairs from the third to the second floor. "There have been many footsteps," Mrs. Graves admits, "but I've pinned most of them down to physical sources. Once our dog got locked up in the playroom above our bedroom, for instance.

"Mostly, you hear them when you are alone. The house does make very strange sounds. There are all sorts of creaks and groans and sways, but it's an old house and you should expect a lot of that. Also, I'm told there's an underground rock ledge and everytime a train goes over it, things rattle and rumble all over town. Still, there are times when your imagination can wander."

Tom Graves is more positive about it. "He's there," he says. "I can't hear as well as my wife, so I haven't heard the footsteps, but I have felt a certain 'presence' in the house. There's definitely some form of psychic phenomena involved."

Another who has experienced the spiritual manifestations is Dr. Paschall, who lived in the house from 1960 through 1971.

Now retired and living in Charles City County, Dr. Paschall says, "I wish I knew some reference as to the origins of the story. I heard it from some of the oldtimers in Williamsburg when I moved in."

Dr. Paschall says he had at least two specific "encounters" with the ghost during his stay in the house, and there were several other times when he thought he heard footsteps on the third floor. "Once, my wife and I were awakened around three in the morning by what we believed were steps. It was something on the stairs moving downward. It was very clear to us, and it was a very unusual feeling. Then it stopped as abruptly as it began.

"Another time, my wife and I were watching TV in our upstairs bedroom when we distinctly heard the front door close. It's a heavy door, and there was no mistaking the sound. We called down to see if our son or daughter had come in. But no one was there. We looked out the back window, but no one had left the house. It was a strange sensation."

Neither Dr. Paschall nor the Graves can offer any explanation as to why the spirit of the French soldier has remained in the house. Likewise, the odd inscription on the bedroom window, the closet door and the mystery of the skeleton pressed into the brick remain unsolved puzzles to this day.

6. The Legend of Lady Skipwith

The George Wythe (rhymes with Smith) House on the west side of Palace Green is a solid brick mansion that is one of the restored showpieces of Colonial Williamsburg. Built during the middle of the 18th century, the house, along with its outbuildings and gardens form what has been described as a "plantation layout in miniature."

The man for whom the house was named was one of the most famous colonists of his day, although he never received the widespread historic recognition of many of his contemporaries. His public career spanned a half-century and he was a leading force in the American struggle for independence. Wythe, it is said, influenced Thomas Jefferson more than any other man. Jefferson, in fact, referred to him as "my faithful and beloved Mentor in youth, and my most affectionate friend through life."

Wythe House

Wythe died tragically in 1806 as a result of being poisoned, allegedly by a grand nephew who thought he would become heir to a fortune. Wythe, however, lived long enough to write the young man out of his will. This incident occurred not at Wythe House, but in Richmond, so there are no reported hauntings of Wythe's spirit in Williamsburg.

There is, nevertheless, a rather well known ghost in the residence; one who has been glimpsed and heard at various times over the two centuries. This would be Lady Ann Skipwith, the daughter of a Scottish merchant. Born near Petersburg about 1741, she was described by those who knew her as an "attractive yet temperamental young woman of a disposition something uncommon." More candidly interpreted, she had a fiery temper and preceded today's women's rights advocates by more than 200 years by frequently speaking her mind. As one early suitor wrote chauvenistically in his diary: "She had a haughtiness, I may even say a fierceness in her countenance which on any little emotion destroyed in some degree that pretty softness which is so amiable in a young lady."

She married Sir Peyton Skipwith, a wealthy planter, and settled down to a comfortable aristocratic life at Prestwould in Mecklenburg County. Once, in the waning days of Williamsburg's glory in the 1770s, before the Colonial capital was moved to Richmond in 1780, Sir Peyton and Lady Ann attended a gala ball at the Governor's Palace. She was resplendent in a cream satin dress and tiny, high heeled red slippers, "upon which shone buckles of brilliants."

But something happened at the ball — no one is quite sure just what — which triggered Lady Ann's famous temper. Offended by whatever slight it was, she bolted from the Palace unescorted even as the minuets continued, and dashed across the Palace Green toward Wythe House. Why she chose this site for her hasty departure remains unexplained, although she may have been a house guest. Whatever, Lady Ann storytellers agree that while enroute she broke either the strap or heel of one of her slippers and arrived at the house hobbling on one shoe, with the other foot clad only in a silk stocking. Thus, she ascended the wooden stairs

sounding somewhat like a person with a peg leg.

It is at this point where the accounts of past writers and actual history part company. According to those who have chronicled the story, including Margaret DuPont Lee, who wrote "Virginia's Ghosts" in 1930, Lady Ann then, in a fit of rage, took her own life. The writers contend she was insanely jealous that Sir Peyton cared more for her sister, Jean, than for her, and what happened at the ball was the last straw. They also wrote that Lady Ann lived in Wythe House at the time, and she now is buried in the small graveyard at nearby Bruton Parish Church.

Researchers at Colonial Williamsburg, however, say the facts are otherwise. Sir Peyton and Lady Ann never lived in Wythe House, although they could have visited there. She did not commit suicide. Rather, she died in childbirth in 1779. And she is not buried at Bruton Parish. Elizabeth Hill Skipwith, wife of Sir Peyton's brother, Henry, lies in rest there.

What the researchers cannot refute, however, is that Wythe House today is haunted with what is most commonly believed to be the spirit of Lady Ann. For nearly 200 years, a number of past residents, visitors, servants and Colonial Williamsburg employees have reported experiencing strikingly similar psychic phenomena in the house.

The most frequent occurrence, almost always at midnight, is the distinct clicking sound of one high heeled slipper on the shallow steps of the broad stairway, alternating with the soft tread of a bare foot. Yet when the stairs and upstairs rooms are searched, no one is ever found. Even today, long time employees speak of such "visitations" in hushed, respectful tones.

Others have witnessed "a beautiful woman, fully gowned in colonial ball costume, to come out of a closet in a certain room, look at herself in a mirror and finally pass out of the door" to vanish. No rational explanation for this often repeated sighting has ever been offered.

The gnawing question is if, in fact, this is the spectral reappearance of Lady Ann Skipwith, why does she return to haunt? Was her jealousy over 200 years ago warranted? One telling clue may lie in what occurred after she died. Sir Peyton did, indeed, marry Lady Ann's sister, Jean!

7. The Gray Lady of Sherwood Forest

One of the most impressive of the plantation houses fronting the James River along the historic corridor in Charles City County which connects Williamsburg with Richmond via Route 5, is Sherwood Forest. Standing on a magnificent 1,600 acre estate in the midst of a towering grove of oaks, this rambling, 300-foot-long mansion, built of framed timbers, boasts the unusual distinction of having been owned by two United States Presidents — William Henry Harrison, and his successor in the White House, John Tyler. It has remained in the Tyler family now for nearly 150 years.

Aside from its architectural attractiveness and historic eminence, Sherwood Forest and its grounds apparently are a primary source for the occurrence of strong psychic phenomena. Through the centuries a number of strange and inexplicable things have happened here ranging from a premonition of death that came true, to mystery voices in the night, to the bizarre slaying of a young Civil War soldier. Most prominent of all, however, is the continued occupancy — for perhaps a century and a half or longer — of the mysterious "Gray Lady," a persistent spirit who walks through certain parts of the house and often rocks in an invisible rocking chair in the wee hours of the morning.

First called the Creek Plantation, the house was built around 1730 at a point on the James River opposite Brandon Marsh. Later, it was owned by Thomas Brown and the property was known as "Tom Brown's Quarter." He, in turn, sold it to a Dr. Rickman, who was surgeon general of the Revolutionary Army. William Henry Harrison inherited it some time after this.

It was President Tyler who named it Sherwood Forest shortly after he bought the house in 1842. He thought the name appropriate since he had been "outlawed" from his Whig party, and also because of the "new green wood" surroundings. Tyler made extensive alterations and renovations to it.

The main part of the house is two and a half stories high, with various passages and wings at different heights. It has been described as a "picturesque old clapboard mansion,"

Sherwood Forest

and features many dormer windows, several chimneys and numerous entrances. Inside, there is a seemingly endless array of rooms, including a private ballroom 68 feet in length. It is said to be the longest house in America of its kind.

Sherwood Forest has been a working plantation for more than 250 years. When Tyler bought it there were 60 to 70 slaves on the estate. His second wife, the vivacious, beautiful, and much younger New York socialite, Julia Gardiner, furnished the interior in a lavish style, importing French mirrors, new rugs and a massive chandelier. The Tylers entertained frequently, and the President, in fact, served his specialty, mint juleps, to visiting heads of state on the plantation's piazza. Formal dinners were served on heirloom porcelain and china, and coffee in private collection demitasse cups to guests seated in petit point chairs.

Today, Sherwood Forest is owned by Harrison Tyler, a grandson of the President, and his wife, Payne. They have made a considerable effort to preserve the historical integrity of the house and grounds, including the reacquisition of many of President Tyler's original artifacts. Group tours can be arranged by appointment, and for an extravagant fee,

Payne Tyler will host group dinners in the presidential dining room, using family silver, porcelain and china.

Whether or not current visitors will experience psychic phenomena during a visit is questionable, although a number of people have through the years. One was Julia Gardiner Tyler herself. When the Civil War broke out in 1861, John Tyler then was in his early seventies. He had worked hard in vain to maintain peace, but once the hostilities began, he sided with his native South and was elected to the Provisional Confederate Congress.

In January 1862, Tyler rode to Richmond, 35 miles away, to attend a conference. Julia and their baby daughter, Pearl, were to join him a week later. Before that could happen, however, Julia had a nightmare in which she envisioned her husband dying in a large bed with a headboard of "a great carved eagle with outstretched wings." She was so upset at the vividness of her dream she went at once to Richmond by carriage. However, he was found perfectly healthy and scoffed at his wife's disturbing vision.

Two days later he suffered an attack at the Exchange Hotel and died in a bed that in detail matched precisely the one Julia had seen in her dream!

As the War between the States progressed, Union troops marched through Charles City County, and for a while General McClelland encamped at Sherwood Forest. He and Tyler had been friends, and McClelland had guards posted around the house to protect it. General Burnside also quartered his men in the "40 acre field" between the house and the James River.

Later, the hated General Butler arrived. Many called him a cruel man, and he often left destruction in his wake. Julia Tyler, fearful of what Butler might do to her family and the estate, took five children and escaped to Wilmington, North Carolina. There, courageously, she ran the Union blockade and traveled north to New York. One Tyler niece and one maid were left at Sherwood Forest.

At this point, the exact details get a little hazy, but there is a legend of a Union soldier — it is not known if he came with Butler or before him — who stood by a kitchen door and tried to set fire to the great house. He was killed before he could succeed, but again, the exact circumstances are in question. One version has it that he was shot in the neck or head by his commanding officer. Another contends that he was struck in the neck or head by someone wielding an ax.

Whatever, more than a century later, Payne Tyler had a woman psychic out to Sherwood Forest, and when the psychic walked up to the kitchen door she froze. She told Payne she felt a definite "coldness" at that spot. "A death has occurred here," she said. "It was a young man and he died with a piece of metal in his head or neck." Payne says the psychic had no way of knowing about the Civil War incident.

As an interesting footnote, General Butler did, in fact, try to burn the house as he left the area. He burned books from Tyler's library, furniture and the wheat fields, and he put lime in the wells. A bale of hay was stacked in the front hall under a table that had been used in the White House and set ablaze as he and his troops rode off. But fate saved the house.

A Union gunboat captain positioned in the James River only a half a mile away saw the smoke. Realizing the historical value of the mansion, he steamed to shore and had his crew put out the fire. He was helped by the maid, who had managed to get some of the hay out of the front hall before a great deal of damage was done.

As to the "mystery voices" at Sherwood, Payne Tyler says they are only heard at night, and usually the summer when the windows are open. "The first time I heard them, I thought it was late night guests," she recalls. "But I looked outside and saw no one." Payne says the voices are always very low and difficult to make out, although once she distinctly heard the voice of a young boy, "about 16 or 17 years old," calling "John."

"Of course, the President's name was John," she says, "but I doubt this was who the voice was referring to. Perhaps it was one of his sons, who also was named John. I do know that others have clearly heard the voices, too, although no one has ever found any explanation for them. We had a gentleman named Anderson occupying an area of the servants' quarter once. One morning he came to me with a funny expression on his face and asked me if I minded if he asked me a very peculiar question. He wanted to know if I ever heard strange voices in the night. He had also heard them."

But all of these assorted incidents are merely preludes to the real spirit of Sherwood Forest — the "Gray Lady."

Precisely how long this lively ghost has inhabited the house is not known, nor is the exact reason why she is there. But it is probably safe to say she has been active since possibly late in the 18th century, long before President John Tyler moved in, because many residents over the years have experienced her presence, and all in the same fashion.

"I wish I could authenticate her origins," says Payne, "but I can't. I can tell you this. She is definitely in the house. I know, because I have personally had encounters with her, as have my husband who was a non-believer in such things, and others."

What Payne has pieced together is that the Gray Lady is called that because she apparently wore gray. This leads to the assumption that she was in the service of the family that owned the house when she lived there, because servants then wore gray when cleaning at Sherwood Forest.

"It is thought that she was a governess, who had charge of a small child at one time here," Payne says. "She would take the child from a first floor bedroom (which is now known, appropriately, as the Gray Room) and walk her up through the hidden staircase to a second floor nursery. There, she would rock the child on her lap in a rocking chair."

Unfortunately, the child was ill and died soonafter. This presents a speculative motive for the Gray Lady's ghost to remain in the house. It could have been that the Gray Lady was not nearby when the child passed away, or she might have perceived that had she been more attentive the tragedy would not have occurred. No one knows for sure.

What is known is that ever since, the sounds of the Gray Lady have been heard in the house — always in the same forms. Her footsteps are heard going up or down the hidden stairway, and the sound of her rocking is heard in the second floor nursery, and in the Gray Room.

"Many people have heard it, and I am one of them,"

Payne unashamedly admits. "The sounds are very distinct and clear. They are footsteps, not creaks or groans of the house. There is an absolute distinction. I have heard the steps or the rocking three separate times since I have been in the house — twice within the first two weeks and once a few months later. Sometimes it sounded like, when she was descending the stairs, she was dragging something. I have no idea what that might have been."

Payne says each time she heard the sounds it was in the early hours of the morning. "What was so peculiar was that I always sleep with two guard dogs who bark at the slightest sound, but for some reason neither one of them stirred at all." When asked if she went to investigate the source, she replied, "are you serious? I was scared out of my wits. It frightened me so. You have no idea of the fear such a thing can evoke. I actually ran a fever."

At first, her husband scoffed at the idea of a ghost. Harrison Tyler is a chemical engineer and a practical man. "He was not a believer in this sort of thing," Payne says. But then it happened to him. "She walked through his bedroom one night," Payne relates. "Harrison turned as white as a sheet and nearly fainted. He even lost his breakfast," she says.

On another occasion, a 16-year-old girl was staying at the house as a guest. She screamed — Payne says "I never heard such a shriek" — and came running in to say she had just heard a woman walk through her room.

Then there was an incident with a gardener. Payne was working in the yard and asked him to hand her a trowel. It lay only a few feet away, but the man refused to go directly to it. Instead, he walked all the way around the 300-foot-long house. When Payne scolded him for taking so long, he stammered something about not wanting to walk past a door that he said was being opened and closed by some invisible person. The gardener then abruptly left the Tyler's employ, still mumbling, almost incoherently, about "ghosts."

After her third experience with the Gray Lady, Payne had had enough. "I know this sounds ridiculous," she says, "but I sat down and had a talk with her. I felt it was something I had to do." What Payne did — and what other people have done

Gray Room at Sherwood Forest

in similar circumstances — was tell the ghost that Sherwood Forest had been in the Tyler family since the 1840s, and descendents had every right to move in and claim the house as their own. If the ghost had designs on the house of her own, that was fine, too, as long as they could peacefully co-exist. "I said, maybe you feel I am an intruder and that this is your domain, but that's not the case and I'm not moving out. We're just going to have to learn to get along together," Payne said.

The frank discussion must have had a positive effect, because Payne has not heard from the Gray Lady since, except for one incredible incident. "That was when a cousin of Harrison's was over for a visit," Payne says, "and I told her about the little talk I had with the spirit. She laughed, and chided me, saying she thought I had more intelligence than that. She just kept laughing. Then the most amazing thing happened. The room we were in, the Gray Room, began vibrating wildly, and there were loud bangs, like shutters slamming against the house. It was an eerie feeling. It so unnerved the woman that she quickly left the house. As soon as she was gone, the vibrations and the noises stopped. She didn't come back for another visit for three or four years."

Intrigued by all that had happened, Payne Tyler, some-time later, was visited by two psychic experts, separately, to go through the house and give her their impressions. One said she saw a "tiny woman in an off-color dress with an apron and black shoes, at the top of the stairs on the second floor. It was decidedly not an apparition, but a real woman. The woman disappeared as the psychic climbed up the stairs.

Interestingly, the other psychic reported experiencing the same phenomena. She said she saw a tiny woman at the top of the stairs "in a neutral dress with an overlay down the front (an apron?) and black shoes." Payne believes they both saw the same woman. This psychic, however, followed the woman into a bedroom and observed her sorting clothes in front of a wardrobe. She described it explicitly as an Empire wardrope, dark brown, with a wide flange at the center, a large brass strip, and having the design of dolphins at each foot.

"When she told me this I was stunned," says Payne. "Julia Tyler was enamored with dolphins and this was the exact description of a piece of furniture that had been in the house, but had been removed two years earlier. It had never been mentioned in any literature about the house, and it had never been photographed. The psychic had no way of knowing it had ever been there, much less what it looked like down to the precise detail."

8. The Devil at Dancing Point

There is, in Charles City County, a spit of land bordering the James River on which, oddly, nothing will grow. Nothing has grown on this particular patch of ground for centuries, yet all the area around it is fertile and productive. The site is known as Dancing Point, and it is said it remains barren because the Devil once danced there.

"Rubbish," you say? "Do you expect any intelligent person to believe a cock-eyed yarn like that?" "The Devil indeed!"

But don't scoff too much or laugh too hard. So maybe you don't believe the legend. Then how, by any sensible means, do you explain the mysterious flickering lights which people have seen eminating from Dancing Point at various times through the decades? And why will nothing grow on this particular parcel of land?

Perhaps you should hear the tale before you make any final judgments. Its origins date to the early days of the Virginia colony in the 17th century. At that time a Colonel Phillip Lightfoot owned land along the James that encompassed Dancing Point. Colonel Lightfoot was from a well-to-do family and is an ancester of Harry Lightfoot Lee and General Robert E. Lee.

Enter the Devil. He claimed a piece of the Lightfoot land was his, and he and the Colonel entered into a bitter dispute over the property. It did not appear that they could resolve it through normal negotiations, so it was suggested they compete in a contest and the winner would claim clear title to the land. It would be a dancing contest.

And so, as it has been faithfully told and retold by generations of Charles City County residents down through the years, the Devil and Colonel Lightfoot marched down to Dancing Point at dusk, shucked their coats and hats, built a roaring fire and began a ritualistic dance to the finish around a large tree stump.

The ceremony continued through the night, with each of them dancing feverishly. Lightfoot, as his name implied, was a highly accomplished hoofer, and as the first rays of the dawning sun pierced the darkness, it was apparent the Devil had met his match. Exhausted and humiliated, Satan, old-timers say, limped away and retreated across the James River to Surry County where he allegedly still lives.

Since that time, more than three centuries ago, the grounds upon which the Devil and Lightfoot tromped have remained bare. And every so often those who have passed by the site in the dead of night have seen flickering flames coming from Dancing Point. Those bold enough to venture nearer have said that if you look closely you can make out the faint silhouettes of two figures circling the fire, their feet working furiously.

9. The Mysterious Fireball at Bacon's Castle

It was, to the Virginia colonists, an ominous sign of impending disaster. It occurred sometime during "the latter months" of the year 1675. A great comet appeared in the sky sweeping across the heavens trailing a bright orange tail of fire. Soonafter this eerie phenomenon came the flight of tens of thousands of passenger pigeons. For days they blanketed the sky, blotting out the sun. Then, in the spring of 1676 a plague of locusts ravaged the colony, devouring every plant in sight and stripping trees of their budding leaves.

But to the colonists, the comet was the worst sign. Many remembered that another comet had streaked across the horizon just before the terrible Indian massacre of 1644. Thus, it was no real surprise to them — because they believed in such spectral omens — when, the following year, one of the bloodiest and most notorious chapters of Virginia history was written.

It began on a quiet summer Sunday when some colonists passing by the Stafford County plantation of Thomas Mathew on their way to church discovered the overseer, Robert Hen, lying in a pool of blood. Nearby lay an Indian servant, dead. Hen also was mortally wounded, but before he expired he managed to gasp, "Doegs! Doegs!" The words struck fear in the hearts of the passersby, for Hen had mentioned the name of a tribe of Indians known for their fierce attacks on white men and women.

The Doeg raid was in retaliation for the killing of several Indians by planters who had caught them stealing pigs and other livestock. Such raids were not new to the colonists. They had been periodically besieged every since they first landed at Jamestown in 1607. But this latest episode proved to be the last straw with many settlers. They had seethed for action for years from the aristocratic governor of the colonies at the time, Sir William Berkeley, but he was reluctant to move.

And so the seeds had been sown for what was to lead to the largest and most violent insurrection of the colonial era to that time — Bacon's Rebellion.

Dashing Nathanial Bacon — 28 years old — had arrived in the colony only three years earlier. Well educated and well endowed, he has been described by biographers as "a slender, attractive, dark-haired young man with an impetuous, sometimes fiery temperament and a persuasive tongue." But perhaps above all else, Bacon was a natural leader of men.

While Governor Berkeley remained inactive and inattentive in Jamestown, planters sought out Bacon to lead retaliatory strikes against the marauding Indians. When his own plantation was attacked and his overseer killed, Bacon agreed. He proved to be a skilled and capable military commander. On one march his forces drove the Pamunkey tribe deep into Dragon's Swamp. Later, Bacon overpowered the Susquehannocks, killing "at least 100 Indians," and capturing others.

Berkeley, furious at the unauthorized attacks launched by this rebellious group, dispatched his own troops to capture Bacon and his men. For the next several weeks the two men waged a cat-and-mouse game that involved daring, intrigue and bloodshed.

At one point Bacon surrendered, was brought before Berkeley and was forgiven when he repented. But then he escaped, returned with a force of 600 men and captured Jamestown, demanding a commision to fight the Indians, as well as a repeal of some harsh colonial laws. With no other choice under the show of arms, Berkeley granted the wishes, but when Bacon set out again chasing Indians, the Governor repudiated all agreements and sent his troops after the rebels.

After several skirmishes, Bacon recaptured Jamestown and had it sacked and burned to the ground. Berkeley, who had retreated to the Eastern Shore of Virginia, meanwhile, was regrouping his forces for a final and decisive confrontation. It never came to pass.

Bacon, who had suffered an attack of malaria at Jamestown, fell critically ill in Gloucester and died of dysentery there on October 26, 1676, at the age of 29. With the leader lost, the rebellion fell apart and Berkeley's forces captured many of Bacon's men. A large number of them were hung, continuing the tragedy forewarned by the appearance of the comet for several more months.

What does all of this have to do with ghosts and psychic phenomena? Read on.

For three months in 1676 about 70 of Bacon's followers occupied a large brick mansion in Surry County, just across the James River from Jamestown. Then called "Allen's Brick House," it has been known, ever since this occupancy, as "Bacon's Castle."

Now operated by the Association for the Preservation of Virginia Antiquities, this imposing brick structure was built some time after 1655. It stands amidst a large grove of oaks. There are two expansive, paneled first floor rooms, two more rooms on the second floor, and what has been described as a "dungeon-like" attic on the third.

According to sketchy historical accounts, the force of Bacon's men who occupied the house during the days of the rebellion was a rowdy one because they were chronicled at the time as "ransacking and making what havoc they

Bacon's Castle

pleased. . ." Such carryings on, however, ceased abruptly two evenings after Christmas 1676, when their surrender was demanded by Captain Robert Morris of the British ship "Young Prince." Noting the size of Morris' force, the rebels decided discretion was the better part of valor and they stole away into the woods at night.

Accounts of hauntings at the castle have been passed along, generation to generation, for more than 300 years now. Many of those who have experienced strange sightings, noises, and "presences," believe they are manifestations of the devil. Others have felt it may be the spectral returning of Bacon's men, still seeking a redressing of the grievances they held against Governor Berkeley and the Colony so many years ago. Whatever, it is undisputed fact that the psychic phenomena that has occurred at the castle through the centuries has taken many forms.

Consider the revelations of Mrs. Charles Walker Warren, whose family once owned the castle. When she was a young woman, early in the 20th century, a visiting Baptist preacher who was spending the night, stayed up late reading his Bible. Sometime in the wee hours of the morning he heard footsteps descending the stairs from the second floor. Someone or something, he said later, opened the parlor door and walked past him. He saw no one, but felt the strong sensation that he was not alone. Then, mysteriously, a red velvet-covered rocking chair began moving back and forward as if someone were sitting in it, though the preacher could see no one. He put down his bible and shouted "get thee behind me Satan," and the rocking stopped immediately.

Mrs. Warren and a number of guests reported hearing footsteps on the stairs late at night many times. One guest distinctly heard "horrible moaning" in the attic directly above her bedroom, though she was assured the next morning that no one could have been in the attic.

On another occasion, Mrs. Warren came into the downstairs parlor one morning and found the glass globe from a favorite nickel-plated reading lamp had been shattered into tiny fragments, yet, strangely, not a drop of kerosene from it had spilled onto the carpet. Also, a leather-bound dictionary had been "flung" across the room onto a sofa, and the iron stand upon which it normally rested had been hurled to a distant corner. No rational explanation could be offered to clear up this happening.

These and several other incidents, however, serve as merely preambles to the most shocking ghostly appearance at Bacon's Castle; one that reappears regularly at varying intervals over the years and has been seen and documented by a number of credible witnesses from several different generations.

It takes the form, say those who have seen it and been terrified by it, of a "pulsating, red ball of fire." It apparently rises near or from the graveyard of Old Lawne's Creek Church a few hundred yards south of the castle, soars about 30 to 40 feet in the air — always on dark nights — and then moves slowly northward. It seems to "float or hover" above the castle grounds before slowly moving back toward the ivy-covered walls of the ruins of Lawne's Creek Church, where it disappears.

One eyewitness, G. I. Price, a former caretaker at the castle, described the phenomenon to a local newspaper reporter in this manner: "I was standing, waiting in the evening for my wife to shut up the chickens, when a light about the size of a jack-me-lantern came out of the old loft door and went up a little . . . and traveled by, just floating along about 40 feet in the air toward the direction of the old graveyard."

Skeptics, of course, contend that the fireball is merely some form of physical manifestation that can be explained scientifically. But those who have seen it, including members of the Warren family and others, could never be convinced that it was not of a mystical, spiritual nature. Some even called it an appearance of the "Prince of Darkness."

One guest reportedly had "the wits frightened out of him" one night when the fiery red ball sailed into his bedroom at the castle, circled over his bed several times and then disappeared out the open window. A former owner of the castle told of seeing the fireball blaze overhead and enter his barn. Fearful of it igniting his stored hay, he ran toward the barn. Then the bright, glowing light turned and headed back

toward the graveyard. In the 1930s, members of a local Baptist church, meeting at an evening revival session, collectively saw the strange sphere. It is said the praying that night was more intense than ever before in the congregation's memory.

What is the origin of this eerie fireball and why does it reappear every so often? One legend has it that a servant a century or so ago was late with his chores and as he was walking home in the darkness the red object overcame him, burst, and "covered him with a hellish mass of flames," burning him to death.

Many oldtimers, however, prefer to believe that the fire-ball is a periodic reminder of the brilliant comet that flashed across the same skies more than 300 years ago, forewarning that tragedy and bloodshed would soon follow. There are, in fact, those who are convinced that spirits frequent Bacon's Castle to this day; sad spirits from long ago, still seeking relief from their troubled and grief-stricken past.

10. Lost Love at Edgewood

There is a hidden aura of brooding sadness that lays, like the shadow of a great oak, across the land that is called Berkeley, a few miles west of Williamsburg in Charles City County. The Berkeley Plantation today is one of the most famous in the world; a beautiful example of colonial Georgian architecture at its finest.

But the historic lore of the area far pre-dates the brick mansion built in the mid 18th century. In fact, it was in the year 1618 — only 11 years after the first settlers landed nearby at Jamestown — that the London Company gave a large grant of land bordering the James River to Sir William Throckmorton, Sir George Yeardley, Richard Berkeley and John Smith. A year later, when 35 settlers arrived from Bristol, England, the new "Town and Hundred of Berkeley" was formed.

It was there that, tragically, on Good Friday 1622, a band of marauding Indians stormed the fragile settlement and killed nine people at Berkeley. That same day, many other settlers at Martin's Hundred also were slain by Indians. For years afterward, the 8,000 or so acres of Berkeley Hundred were abandoned.

It was not until 1636 that the "white men" reclaimed the site. It eventually became the property of John Bland, a merchant of London. His son, Giles Bland, was a favored lieutenant of the rebellion leader Nathanial Bacon, and when Bacon's insurrection collapsed in 1676, Bland was ordered hanged by Governor Sir William Berkeley.

The property then came into the possession of Benjamin Harrison III whose ancestors were from Wakefield. His son was the builder of the present house. In turn, his son, Benjamin Harrison V, a signer of the Declaration of Independence, inherited the house in 1744. It was under his tenure that the plantation flourished. He owned and operated a grist mill for grinding corn and wheat on the site's 17,000 acres. Water was supplied by a large lake via a mile long canal dug by slaves. Stones for the mill were shipped from the Alps of Italy.

Amidst all the tragic past of Berkeley, it would seem to be a fertile ground for the ghosts of grief-stricken early settlers, or perhaps at least for the maligned spirit of Giles Bland. But such is not the case. There is a ghost who frequents the neighboring land, but the legend behind its origins is not directly associated with the Berkeley mansion itself, nor is it tied into the bloodshed which once soaked the historic grounds there.

Rather, it is the gentle, romantic spirit of a young woman, still searching vainly for her lost lover. She is Miss Elizabeth "Lizzie" Rowland, once mistress of Edgewood. Located just a quarter of a mile from Berkeley, directly on Route 5, Edgewood is a three story Gothic home with 12 rooms, 10 fireplaces and five chimneys. Inside is a beautiful winding three story stairway, original lustrous wide pine floors, original Gothic windows and a large country kitchen.

The house was built about 1849 by Spencer Rowland, Lizzie's father. It was also referred to as Roland's Mill. About 80 yards from the house, still standing, is an old mill which was part of the Berkeley Plantation, dating back to the early

Edgewood

1800s. Here, one may see massive hand-hewn timbers, huge mill stones and the canal, or mill race, which was dug by slave labor and extends to Harrison Lake a mile away. It is said that Confederate General Jeb Stuart stopped at Edgewood on June 15, 1862, for a cup of coffee before continuing on his famous ride around McClellan's forces.

Lizzie was Spencer Rowland's only daughter, and her tombstone can be found today in nearby Westover churchyard. The inscription reads: "Elizabeth Rowland, born May 20, 1823...died Feb. 6, 1870...Dear Sister How We Love Thee."

The details of Lizzie's love affair have grown faint through the years. Little is known of her gentleman admirer except that he apparently lived on an adjacent plantation, perhaps Berkeley, and often could be heard approaching Edgewood on what has been described as his "spirited horse." Lizzie would rush to a front bedroom window whenever she heard the hoof beats. Then her lover left her to go off to battle during the Civil War, never to return.

Thus Lizzie died a few years later, a saddened maiden. But her spirit apparently lives on at Edgewood, still hoping for her lover to come back. A number of witnesses have declared seeing the frail spectre of Lizzie peering from behind the curtains of an upstairs window. She usually is dressed in white and holds a candle. To those who have watched in revered silence, it appears that the apparition passes from window to window. Subsequent searches of the house, however, reveal no trace of anyone.

"Oh, her presence definitely still is in the house," says Dot Boulware, current owner of Edgewood. "I've experienced her a number of times personally, and so have many visitors. When my husband and I first bought the house in 1978, we heard a legend that Lizzie had etched her name in a bedroom window, but previous owners had never been able to find it. One day my son was cleaning the windows in the bedroom where she had died — the windows were so filthy you could hardly see out of them — when he screamed at me. There, in the upper left hand corner of the bottom pane, we saw her name delicately etched in the glass."

A number of eerie incidents have happened to Dot at Edgewood. "We've had pictures fall off the walls, and once a heavy ornamental cannon fell off a mantle. There is no way it could have fallen on its own. We think Lizzie was upset at something and knocked it off. Another time a fire started in one of the upstairs rooms without apparent cause. Even the insurance man couldn't figure out what started it. At other times we've found the front door wide open after it had been locked."

Dot says once an old woman came to tour through the house and when they got to the second floor, she stopped cold at the entrance to Lizzie's bedroom. "She turned to me and said, 'honey, do you know this house is haunted?' She said she had a strong extra sensory perception and she felt strong vibrations. When I told her about the pictures and the cannon falling, she said it was because when Lizzie's boy-friend went off to war he went by sailing ship, one that had cannon on its decks. But she also told me Lizzie's spirit likes me and I am in no danger.

"Another time," Dot continues, "a psychic came to visit after she had heard about the ghost of Edgewood. She took a candle in a bowl when she explored the rooms, and wherever she said she felt the presence of Lizzie, the flame grew brighter, her hands got very cold and the room became frigid. This woman had never seen the house before, but she went right to the window pane where Lizzie had sketched her name."

Occasionally, Dot and her husband host weddings at Edgewood. In fact, the house was used for church services during the Civil War when nearby Westover Church was stabling Union horses. After one such wedding, Dot and some friends were looking over the photographs taken of the occasion, when someone exclaimed, "look at the upper window." There, it appeared a frail woman was looking out.

"There is no way anyone could have been in that room at the time," Dot says, "because when we have a wedding we store all the parlor furniture in that room, and it's wall to wall. No human being could have gotten through it all to that window. It must have been Lizzie!"

But of all the incidents which have happened at Edgewood since Dot has owned it, the most frightening occurred one evening when she and her husband were hosting a dinner party for 12 couples. "After dinner the men all went into another room and we all stayed in the dining room, chatting. The talk got around to Lizzie and I began telling them about her, when one of the women said, 'that's all a lot of baloney. There are no ghosts.' Just then a brass plate that had been atop a cabinet suddenly fell off and hit the woman on the head. Everyone was stunned into silence, and within a few minutes everyone had left. They were all visably shaken."

And so, it seems, according to Dot Boulware and many others, Lizzie continues to stand her lonely vigil, in the never-dying hope that she will once again glimpse the sight of her lost beau bounding across the grounds on his robust steed, coming at last to claim the love that was lost in life.

11. Indian Spirits at Brafferton

It is altogether fitting that the athletic teams of the College of William and Mary — the second oldest institution of higher learning in the United States — are called the "Indians." It is fitting because in the late 17th and 18th centuries Indians native to the area routinely roamed through the campus woods and grounds which today are lined with modern classroom facilities, administrative buildings and dormitories.

It is fitting because in those days so long ago some of the young braves exhibited physical prowess worthy of the finest skills of the College's varsity athletes today. In fact, it is upon the specific extraordinary abilities of one such Indian boy that a local legend has been built; one that has grown steadily stronger through the years. It is fueled by belief of many Williamsburg townspeople that the ghost of this sad and homesick boy occasionally still can be seen running across the great campus — with the grace and effortless style of a deer — in the dark mist of early morning hours.

It was late in the 17th century, when the college and the colony were in their infancies, that another school was founded in Williamsburg. Its purpose was to train Indian boys in the fineries of civilization, and teach them the intricacies of the English language. The boys were sent to the area and boarded with local farmers and other colonists.

It was a hard and difficult time for the young lads. Used to romping unencumbered in the woods, they found the restraints and restrictions of civilized school life in a structured community harsh and confining. They were heartbroken and homesick. They longed to return to their families and villages. Instead, they were forced into a strict environment, often with strangers who understood neither their customs or their feelings.

In some cases they were treated cruelly and inhumanely by colonists whose friends and relatives had been killed or injured in Indian raids during the early settlement days in Virginia. On the streets, they were taunted and jeered by the young sons of colonists. At school, they found the lessons

Brafferton Building

arduous and demanding, the language confusing. They felt lost and unwanted.

Compounding their problems, the Indian boys were fed a diet that consisted largely of pork and corn meal. Many of them contracted a TB vacillus, and a number of them died, both from physical and psychological reasons. This caused a scandal and improvements were demanded.

So it was that early in the 18th century a new building was erected for the Indians. It was called the Brafferton Building and it was built in 1723 from an endowment of the English scientist Robert Boyle, who wished "to bring the gospel to the Indians."

The rooms were large and airy for the day, and it was hoped, by boarding the boys here, the morale problem could be solved. For a while, under the astute guidance of a headmaster named Griffin, it was. But then he died an untimely death and things got worse.

Soon, the building was filled with unhappy boys again. Most of their fathers had been killed, and many of them were captured and brought to Williamsburg against their desires. They were from several tribes and had trouble understanding and adjusting even to each other. Many boys tried to escape, and they had to be locked into the building each night. They were forced to wear a uniform — a scratchy green wool suit.

It is from this tragic background that the hauntings of Brafferton House and the legend of the gifted Indian boy athlete have emerged. The use of the house as a residence for the young braves was discontinued in 1736, but the sad spirits of those who died there apparently transcend the centuries and live on.

For many people have reported hearing strange sounds at Brafferton in the dead of night. Such sounds have included faint footsteps, woeful moans, and sobbing. Yet, repeated investigations through the house have turned up no physical cause for them.

One who has personally experienced the "rumblings" of restless spirits in Brafferton is Wilford Kale, for many years the Williamsburg bureau chief for the Richmond Times-Dispatch. In the mid-1960s he lived for a summer on the third floor of the house while he worked at the College of William and Mary.

"I definitely heard some sounds that summer which you could describe as psychic phenomena or whatever you want to call it," Kale says. "I know they didn't come from any known source because I couldn't find any explanation for them."

On more than one occasion Kale distinctly heard the sound of footsteps shuffling around on the third floor. Each time it was late at night and he was alone in the building. "The sound was very clear," he recalls. "It was someone walking around. It wasn't any shutter banging or boards creaking. Each time I got up to look, but I never saw anything."

What unnerved Kale the most, however, was the night when he heard what he describes as "the beating of Indian tom toms." Again, the sounds came when he was alone. "I was asleep and I was awakened by this rhythmic beat on drums. I sat up straight in bed. It must have gone on for a minute or a minute and a half. I got up and went into the hallway. Then I walked down to the first floor and back up again, but I saw nothing. It was a spooky feeling."

As to the young Indian athlete, no one knows his name, or where he came from. Nothing is known of his family or the particular circumstances which led him to the melancholy life he suffered at the school.

But his was an uncommon spirit of independence. He hated the building and the confinement. He longed for the great expances of the outdoors. So, he concealed a rope and smuggled it to his room on the third floor. There, late at night he climbed down the rope from a hall window and, bare breasted, ran through the woods which surrounded the College of William and Mary. How he loved to run; it was his escape, his brief, fleeting time of freedom. To those who glimpsed him in the dark, he seemed to run with the ease and endurance of a long distance racer. He would run for hours,

often to the point of exhaustion. And then he would return before dawn and climb back up the rope to his room.

Word passed through the community of this boy and his nocturnal journeys, but few saw him and no one ever came close to catching him. One night he collapsed, and when his fallen form was discovered he was dead. No one knows how he died, but some speculate it was from a broken heart. Others have said he was shot by someone who laid in wait for him.

Nevertheless, his legend has lived on, because for more than 250 years students at the college have reported seeing a fleeting figure dash across the grounds late at night in the dampened mist. There have been scores of such sightings through the years.

What actually is seen, say oldtimers, is the spirit of the sad Indian boy, still seeking the freedom that was denied him so long ago.

12. "Mad Lucy" of Ludwell-Paradise House

Some called her, perhaps too generously, eccentric, capricious, whimsical or odd. Others just said she was crazy. Whatever, it is certain that she was one of a kind, and her curious behavior caused excited titters of whispered gossip in the upper strata of 18th century social circles on two continents.

It is probable that had she not been from a well-to-do family, she might have been committed to a mental institution early on in her life. As it was, her actions were covered up, embarrassingly laughed off, or otherwise explained away as those of a high strung young lady with a flair for being mischievious.

She was Lucy Ludwell, second daughter of Philip Ludwell III. She married John Paradise, a scholar and linquist and an accepted member of the intellectual set which, in those days, surrounded the eminent Dr. Samuel Johnson. Lucy lived

Ludwell-Paradise House

much of her life in London, and, according to one published account, "startled London society by such exploits as dashing boiling water from her tea urn on a too garrulous gentleman who annoyed her."

Earlier in the 18th century her grandfather had built a town residence in Williamsburg — a handsome brick mansion that was called "architecturally sophisticated" for its day. Surrounding the main house are stables, a paddock, a well, smokehouse, "necessary" house, and a woodhouse close to the kitchen. A garden features a prized dwarf boxwood collection.

Property Lucy inherited in Virginia was confiscated by the Commonwealth during the Revolutionary War, because the politics espoused by her husband were alien to the cause of the colonists fighting for their freedom. In 1805, however, 10 years after her husband died, Lucy set sail for America and was allowed to take up residence in what has become known as Ludwell-Paradise House.

It was here, as she got along in age, that she again became the talk of the town with her peculiar habits. For openers, Lucy, because of her social position in London, considered herself "above" her friends and neighbors in Virginia. She had a haughty attitude which she made no effort to disguise. It is said she "held court" at her house, and didn't object in the least to being called "Madame."

She also was impulsive and obsessive. Once when the future fifth President of the United States, James Monroe, and his family came to Williamsburg, Lucy startled him by rushing up and declaring, "Sir, we have determined to make you president."

Another of Lucy's quirks was her penchant for borrowing the new clothes of her lady friends, especially hats. She viewed herself as a fashion plate of the times and seemed oblivious to the fact that everyone in town knew when she was donning loaned clothing. On Sundays the congregation at her church always got a chuckle because Lucy regularly had her "little black boy" — a servant's son — carry her prayer book into church ahead of her, as if to announce her imminent entrance.

Mad Lucy is probably best remembered for entertaining guests on weird carriage rides. They were weird in that they never went anywhere. She had a favorite coach reassembled on the back porch of her house. When callers dropped by she would invite them into the coach and then have it rolled back and forth across the porch on imaginary trips by a servant.

Her fantasy carriage rides became so frequent and her other peculiarities so pronounced that Lucy began having difficulty differentiating between the worlds of make-believe and reality. Eventually, in 1812, she was committed to the state asylum.

While Lucy died two years later, her spirit apparently remains entrenched in the Ludwell-Paradise House. A number of occupants have reported hearing strange sounds there unattributable to any known physical source. Most notable of the witnesses are Mr. and Mrs. Rudolph Bares. Bares is a retired vice president of Colonial Williamsburg who lived in the house for several years in the 1960s and 1970s.

"Oh, we never heard any ghostly voices, saw any levitations or anything like that," Bares says. "But my wife and I each experienced the same odd phenomenon on several different occasions, maybe eight, 10 or 12 separate times. And that is we would be downstairs when we would hear the water running in a second floor bathtub. Then we would hear a splashing sound in the tub, as if someone were taking a bath.

"The first few times we heard it, we went up the stairs to take a look, but there was never anything or anyone there, and no water was running in the tub. So after a while we wouldn't even check when we heard it. We'd just laugh and say it must be Lucy pouring a bath for herself."

Cleanliness, it should be noted, was another of Mad Lucy's idiosyncracies. She was known to often have taken several baths a day.

13. The Trapped Soldier of Nelson House

Had not fate intervened, chances are few people, other than local residents, would ever have heard of the sleepy, peaceful little town of Yorktown, Virginia, about 15 miles to the northeast of Williamsburg. But destiny stepped in more than 200 years ago, indelibly inscribing Yorktown as a prominent name in American history books.

It was here, during a few days in October 1781, that General George Washington, commander of the American Armies, outmaneuvered General George Cornwallis and defeated his once-proud British forces during a furious siege which, for all practical purposes, brought an end to the Revolutionary War.

Today, Yorktown remains a relatively quiet town, its peacefulness interrupted each summer by thousands of tourists who walk the hallowed battle grounds, upon which America's independence was courageously won so many years ago.

Not everyone remembers. In fact, if you ask about for the most famous landmark in Yorktown now, you're likely to be told it's Nick's Seafood Pavillion, a local restaurant that has gained a widespread reputation for the variety and freshness of its ample servings of everything from flounder stuffed with crabmeat, to Chesapeake Bay oysters which slept on the floor of the sea the previous evening.

If you ask history buffs about area landmarks, however, they will undoubtedly point to an imposing brick house perched high on a hill overlooking the York River. Here, standing majestically more than 250 years since its erection, is the Nelson House, sometimes referred to as York Hall.

Its personal history intertwines inexorably with the growing pangs of a young nation struggling for its freedom. It played an interesting part in the final battle at Yorktown, and therein lies a ghostly legend that has survived the centuries. For it is said that Nelson House is haunted by the spirit of a British soldier who was killed during the final fighting in 1781 by an ironic twist of luck.

The house itself, according to Clyde F. Trudell, author of

Nelson House

"Colonial Yorktown," was begun in 1711 and completed some years later. Trudell says "several travelers described it as early as 1732 in such a manner as would lead us to believe that it was not a new building then."

It was built on a terrace, surrounded by a garden, with a protecting wall, and has been variously described as "a pretentious brick mansion," "Yorktown's most interesting relic," and "a spacious and dignified manor." A massive structure of red brick with stone trim and ivy covered walls on the corner of Main and Nelson Streets, it also has been called "one of the best examples of Georgian architecture in all Virginia."

The house was built by the ancestors of Thomas Nelson, a member of the Continental Congress, Commanding General of the Virginia militia during the Revolutionary War years, a Governor of Virginia, and a signer of the Declaration of Independence.

In the years immediately preceding the war, Thomas Nelson and his bride, the former Lucy Grymes of Brandon,

Va., "entertained all the great dignitaries of the Colony," in their grand house, "becoming themselves the social and political leaders of York County." Margaret DuPont Lee, author of "Virginia Ghosts, wrote: "Many a cheering cup was filled to the brim in the dining room where candles gleamed, while shadows danced on the lovely pine wainscot, now mellowed by age to a beautiful brown."

The Nelson family eventually had to abandon the house when the British occupied Yorktown. In fact, during the final days of the Revolutionary War, Lord Cornwallis, for a time, used the house as his headquarters.

Thus was the setting on the morning of October 9, 1781 when General Washington's men and their allied forces, including artillery, were set strategically in place for the final siege which would forever secure Yorktown's prominent place in American history.

The bombardment began about 3 p.m. As the firing started, General Nelson was asked "to point out a good target toward which the artillerists could direct their fire." Stoically and without hesitation, he pointed to a large brick mansion which he suggested might be serving as Cornwallis' headquarters. The house Nelson indicated was his own. It was a magnificent act of patriotic self sacrifice which greatly impressed Lafayette.

Cannon fire was directed toward the house and several shells directly hit the target. One apparently penetrated a secret stairway hidden behind a panel in the dining room hall leading to a garret. It was here, as local folklore has it, that a British soldier was hiding. He was killed by the blast, and it is his ghost which remains a sad and restless presence in Nelson house to this day.

The house itself remained in the Nelson family until 1907 when it was sold to Joseph Bryan of Richmond. It was later purchased and restored by the late Captain George Preston Blow of LaSalle, Illinois. Most of the war damage to the structure was repaired, although a couple of cannonballs were left in the eastern wall of the building facing Nelson Street as mementoes.

For some years the Blows entertained in the house in a

manner somewhat reminiscent of how the Nelsons had done 150 years or so earlier. It was during one of these socials that the ghost made its most noted "showing." Mrs. Blow was hosting a luncheon for several ladies. One of the guests asked her if the house was haunted. Mrs. Blow answered that when she and her husband bought it they had heard stories of the ghost of a British soldier who had been killed in the Yorktown bombardment in 1781. But, she added, she had not seen or heard anything to substantiate the story during her stay in the house.

Apparently, her disclaimer infuriated the spirit, because, according to eye witness accounts, no sooner had she gotten the words out when the secret door behind the panel in the dining room burst open with "terrific force" which shook the room as if an earthquake had hit. The force knocked against a sideboard with such violence "that several dishes crashed to the floor, shattered beyond repair."

Then, eerily, there was a stony silence and an icy stillness in the room, save for the muffled gasps of the obviously terrified guests. After the briefest of pauses — although it seemed like an eternity to the ladies — Mrs. Blow heroically offered that the inexplicable phenomenon perhaps had been caused by a sudden down draught of air. No one in the room believed her, but fearful of tempting a further display of spiritual force, they offered no resistence when their hostess steered the conversation into more pleasant topics.

Later, Mrs. Blow confided to a friend that, in fact, she had experienced no draught whatsoever, but she could not offer any sane explanation for what she had felt and seen.

In 1968 Nelson House was acquired by the National Park Service. To this day, tour guides, when asked about the legend of the ghost of the British soldier are careful about their comments, fearful that any flat denial of his "existence" might bring on another frightening psychic demonstration.

14. "Discarnate Phantasms" at Greenway

In the psychic vernacular, some people are known as being "mediumistic." In essence, that means certain individuals possess strong "vibes," or whatever you wish to call it, through which spirits communicate. Such persons seem to have a psychic gift, or sense which somehow has been developed to an advanced, sensitive state which enables them to experience spiritual phenomena far beyond the realm of "average" people. No one really knows why this is true, but experts are in general agreement on this point.

That is why, in many instances where a ghost is involved, it will seem to communicate through one member of a family. There are numerous documented cases of this on file. Often, all residents of a house may "feel" a presence in one fashion or another, such as hearing footsteps or other sounds. But only one person sees the apparition or has an understanding of why the ghost is there. If the purpose of the ghost is to convey a message, it is usually done through this individual.

Maria Henry Tyler apparently was such a person. She was a favored daughter of Governor John Tyler, Sr., and the sister of John Tyler, the tenth president of the United States. It is said that as a young girl she was a "pet" of Thomas Jefferson who was a friend and sometimes guest of her father.

Maria grew up at Greenway, a 17th century plantation home near the James River about half a mile from the Charles City County courthouse. It was here that the future president was born and raised. Greenway is not large by plantation home standards, but it is reportedly the second oldest original home in the county, having been built sometime in the second half of the 17th century. It has been described as a "fine example of Colonial architecture." One of the features of this frame house is a "most interesting fireplace" with a hearth laid in bricks made at the site more than three centuries ago.

Surrounding the main, T-shaped house is an 18th century sprawl of outbuildings, including a law office, kitchen, laundry-bakery, smokehouse, icehouse, harness house and slave quarters. Earlier, the property had been known as Marlee, but when one of the Tyler girls remarked about the

Greenway

greenness of the grass and plants surrounding the house, Governor Tyler renamed it Greenway.

It was here that Maria and young John Tyler, the future president, romped as children. And it was here that Maria witnessed — on separate occasions years apart — two "discarnate phantasms."

The first occurred when she was still quite young and living in Greenway. Her mother had died some time earlier. On this particular occasion, Maria was sleeping in a large double bed with a girl friend who had come over for a visit. Across the room in another, smaller bed lay Maria's little sister. After talking themselves out, the girls had finally dropped off to sleep.

It was at some point in the early morning hours that something startled and roused Maria from her deep slumber. Unaware of just what it was, Maria propped herself up on her elbows and blinked her eyes. The room was bathed in bright moonlight streaming through a window and she could see things quite clearly. Some unseen force seemed to draw her gaze toward the bed of her sister, and in so doing, Maria gasped. For there, bending over the side of her sister's bed was the distinct image or vision — Maria was to call it a discarnate phantasm — of her dead mother!

Maria was stunned but not afraid. According to Anne Tyler Netick, a descendent of the Tyler family and now an associate professor of Russian at the College of William and Mary, Maria observed the apparition for several seconds in silence. Her girl friend, however, also had been awakened and upon seeing the same thing exclaimed, "Maria, there is your mother!" At the sound of her voice the phantasm disappeared without a trace before their eyes. Maria and her friend often told of the incident, and, in fact, the bedroom in which it took place has since been known as the haunted chamber.

Many years later, after Maria had married and moved on in life, she was back visiting at Greenway during a period when it was owned by her brother. One night during her stay one of the young Tyler children was taken seriously ill, and, Netick says, Maria was helping care for him. Something was needed from the haunted chamber and Maria, without a thought about the vision she had seen there years earlier, went into the room to get it.

There, once again, her breath was taken from her, for standing before her was a phantasm of her father, Governor John Tyler, Sr., who had died some years before. He was wearing a familiar suit of brown clothes and presented such a vivid image to Maria that she was able to see his birthmark — a large mole on his forehead.

She stood stark still, as did he, as their eyes met. Her heart raced. She dared not speak. But just as before, a voice broke the eerie spell. Her sister in law in a downstairs room called out to her, "Maria, Maria," and the vision of her father immediately vanished.

15. The Puzzling Riddle of the Refusal Room

It has been described by many as the most beautiful house in America. Indeed, the stately Georgian mansion, shaded by a row of enormous old tulip poplar trees overlooking the scenic James River, is a magnificent building even though it is nearly 250 years old. Carter's Grove, in James City County, Virginia, near Newport News, is rich in history.

Construction of the house itself began in 1750 on a beautiful 1,400 acre tract of land bought by the legendary Virginia colonist Robert "King" Carter, one of the wealthiest and most influential men of his time. At his death he was said to have been owner of more than 300,000 acres of land and over 1,000 slaves. He chose the site for the benefit of his daughter, Elizabeth Carter.

The kitchen was built first, followed by an office at the end of the west wing. "King" Carter died before the building was completed, willing it to Elizabeth's son, Carter Burwell. He also specified that it "in all times to come be called and to go by the name of Carter's Grove." It was Burwell who added the

Carter's Grove

main house, hiring the finest brick masons and carpenters in the area.

In 1752, Burwell paid the passage to America of an English artisan, Richard Baylis. For three years this skilled craftsman worked and supervised the work of others in carving and installing the splendid woodwork that is the pride of Carter's Grove.

The house and grounds today are part of a historic foundation and are open to the public. Tens of thousands of tourists visit the plantation each year, marveling at its beauty. Guides carefully explain the background of the house, describe its elaborate period furnishings, and tell of the many famous guests who visited centuries ago. It was a showpiece residence and many lavish and memorable parties and dinners were held here for rich and famous personages of 18th century Virginia.

Like other plantation homes along the James River, Carter's Grove has its share of colorful legends and anecdotes. There are, for example, deep scars in the handsome hand-hewn stair railing leading up from the front hall on the first floor. These were said to have been made during the Revolutionary War by a British cavalryman, Colonel Banastre Tarleton, who rode his horse up the stairway, "hacking the balastrade with his sabre as he ascended."

And if ever there was a site "ripe" for spiritual hauntings of unrestful souls, it would be Carter's Grove. That's because on the grounds is the site at which a great tragedy occurred more than 350 years ago. Here, archeologists searching for 18th century artifacts, uncovered the remnants of a colony of early settlers dating back to the year 1619. The settlement was known as Martin's Hundred, and all residents of it were massacred by Indians in 1622.

Through the years there have been "occurrences" at the plantation site which leads one to believe psychic phenomena is involved. There is, for instance, the story told by husband and wife caretakers who were alone at the estate one evening. While doing chores in different parts of the west end of the mansion, each distinctly heard "footsteps" eminating from the east end. The man assumed it was his wife, and vice versa.

Later, when they met, they learned to their astonishment that the other had not ventured in the west end of the house. A search revealed nothing.

A supervisor of tour guides tells of an old gardener, now retired, who occasionally heard a woman playing a harp in an upstairs room. No one could ever convince him otherwise, although no known source for the musical interludes was ever found.

But it is a downstairs drawing room of the house that the "real" ghost of Carter's Grove resides. Long time servants at the mansion are convinced that this room is haunted. It was here that a pretty young woman, Mary Cary, allegedly turned down a proposal for marriage in the mid 18th century from an ardent suitor named George Washington. Some years later, in the same room, Thomas Jefferson offered his hand to "fair" Rebecca Burwell. He, too, was rejected. This parlor subsequently became known as the "refusal room."

In the years since, some peculiar things keep reoccurring in the room. Most notably, whenever white carnations are placed in it, they are mysteriously ripped to shreds late at night and scattered about. No one knows who does it or why only white carnations are chosen, and only the ones in the refusal room, whereas other flowers in the house remain untouched.

In 1939, the Associated Press carried a nationwide story on the phenomenon, quoting Mrs. Archibald McCrea, then owner of Carter's Grove. She said at the time that it was true that "something" was coming in at night to "blight her blooms." Traps were set for mice but they were never sprung. John Coleman, an elderly butler, said it was "ghosts."

Tour hostesses at the plantation say occasionally even today they find the shredded petals of white carnations littered about the room. No one at the site, present or past, has offered any semblance of an explanation for such strange phenomena. It also is highly doubtful that the torn petals are the work of a prankster, or a succession of pranksters because when the house is open tour guides are always in or near the room, and when the house is closed at night, security guards keep a close watch and there are alarm systems throughout

Refusal Room at Carter's Grove

which would be triggered by anyone prowling about.

Could it thus be the spirit of one of the two famous spurned lovers, unable to contain his rage of rejection? If you believe in ghosts, it's possible. But some say it more likely may be the return of one of the women who refused. For it is said that when Mary Cary watched the triumphant Continental Army enter the area after the Yorktown surrender in 1781, commanded by General Washington, she was so overcome by chagrin that she fainted dead away in her husband's arms. So it is speculated that it may be her spirit which sometimes slips into the house late at night to tear the carnations in a fit of anger at which might have been, had she accepted Washington's original bouquet and proposal offer more than two centuries ago.

16. The Triple Ghosts of Westover

Two large metallic eagles adorn the gateposts leading into Westover Plantation, in Charles City County, Virginia, set majestically along a beautiful stretch of the James River. Not as well known as the neighboring Berkeley Plantation, Westover, nevertheless is considered an outstanding example of Georgian architecture in America. Built in the early 18th century, it was, for generations, the ancestral home of the William Byrd family, one of the most powerful and influential clans in the colonies.

The mansion features a steeply sloping roof flanked by tall chimneys in pairs at both ends. A surrounding wrought iron fence has supporting columns topped by unusual stone finials cut to represent: an acorn for perseverance (from little acorns great oaks grow); a pineapple for hospitality; a Green key to the world for knowledge; a cornucopia or horn of plenty; a beehive for industry; grapes for mirth; and an urn of flowers for beauty.

Westover was the scene of lavish social entertainment among the more affluent colonists during the 18th century. Great parties were held there with the rich and famous as frequent guests. But the house also is filled with a history of sadness and tragedy, and for centuries has been haunted by no less than three separate ghosts.

If there is such a thing as a "benevolent" spirit, or at least one who is dedicated not to frighten those who see it, then there is perhaps no better example than the gentle, almost fragile spirit of Evelyn Byrd of Westover. Though she has been dead for nearly 250 years, her apparition still occasionally reappears there; a wraith-like figure most often dressed in white; sad and haunting as if still seeking the happiness which eluded her in life so long ago.

Born in 1707, she was a bright child, a bit spoiled, precocious and high spirited. She was the daughter of William Byrd II, master of Westover and one of the most prominent statesmen of his time; secretary of the Virginia colony for years; advisor to the governor; founder of the city of Richmond; wealthy land owner; and country squire.

Westover

When she was just 10, her father took her to England so she could be properly schooled. There, she flowered into a beautiful young woman with porcelain-white skin, shining chestnut hair, slanting, almost-Oriental blue-green eyes, and an enigmatic, Mona-Lisa-like smile. It is told that when she was presented at court at age 16 the King of England remarked: "I am not surprised why our young men are going to Virginia if there are so many pretty Byrds there."

It was in London that Evelyn fell deeply in love with a handsome Englishman. Most historians believe he was Charles Morduant, the grandson of Lord Peterborough. Her father violently objected to the romance, telling her that if she proceeded with it, "as to any expectation you may fondly entertain of a fortune from me, you are not to look for one brass farthing...Nay besides all that I will avoid the sight of you as of a creature detested."

And so, against the desires of her heart, Evelyn Byrd returned to Westover in 1726 a different young woman. The spark of her personality was diminished and she spent long hours by herself, withdrawn, almost reclusive. A number of potential suitors from nearby plantations paid her visits over the next few years, but she spurned them all, much to the chagrin of her father. He referred to her as the "antique virgin."

She confided only in her close friend, Anne Carter Harrison of nearby Berkeley Plantation. They would walk in the formal gardens and talk among the giant boxwoods, passing the afternoons away. It was amid a poplar grove one day that the two young ladies made a pact. Whichever one died first would try to return to visit "in such a fashion not to frighten anyone." Did Evelyn have a premonition? For soon after, she passed away, some say, of a broken heart.

On her tombstone was inscribed the following: "Here in the sleep of peace reposes the body of Evelyn Byrd, daughter of the Honorable William Byrd. The various and excellent endowments of nature: improved and perfected by an accomplished education formed her, for the happiness of her friends; for the ornament of her country. Alas Reader! We can detain nothing, however valued, from unrelenting death. Beauty, fortune, or valued honour! So here a proof! And be reminded by this awful tomb that every worldly comfort fleets away. Excepting only, what arises from imitating the virtues of our friends and the contemplation of their happiness. To which, God was pleased to call this Lady on the 13th day of November, 1737, in the 29th year of her age."

For months the saddened Anne Harrison did not venture among the trails and trees they had so often walked together. But one day she finally did go to the poplar grove and felt "a presence." She turned and saw a figure approaching. It was Evelyn. She was "dressed in white, dazzling in ethereal loveliness. She drifted forward a few steps, kissed her hand to the beholder, smiling happily, and vanished."

In the intervening generations, many others have caught fleeting glimpses of Evelyn, among them former Westover owners and guests. In 1856, for example, one woman told the John Seldens, who then lived at Westover, that she had awakened in the night and found a young lady standing in the room who quickly went out the door. The woman described the lady and her dress. "Oh, yes," Mr. Selden remarked, "that was Evelyn Byrd." In the 1920s a young girl sleeping in the same third floor bedroom proclaimed the identical experience.

In the early 1900s a workman was dispatched to do some repair work in that bedroom. Minutes later he came running down the stairs saying to the owner, "you didn't tell me there was a young lady up there." He had seen her combing her hair before a mirror. But when they went back upstairs there was no one there.

In December 1929, a guest of the Richard Cranes, who then owned the plantation, reported seeing the "filmy, nebulous and cloudy figure of a woman, so transparent no features could be distinguished, only the gauzy texture of a woman's form." It seemed, the guest said, "to be floating a little above the lawn."

In fact, when the Cranes bought Westover around 1920, Mrs. Crane said, "oh dear, we'll never get any help because of the ghosts." But they had no trouble, because even though the legend of Evelyn's reappearances was known throughout Charles City County, servants also believed her to be a friendly spirit.

And indeed, servants, too, have experienced the phenomenon. One old butler was coming through a narrow passageway in the hall when he saw a lady. Presuming it to be Mrs. Crane, he stepped aside to let her pass. She disappeared before his eyes. Another time a cook saw the apparition of a woman without a head, her view partially blocked by pantry shelves.

More recently, Mr. Bagby, who lives in a small house between the mansion and the cemetary where Evelyn is buried, was in his kitchen one evening when he saw a woman at eye level outside on the lawn. Thinking it was Mrs. Bruce Crane Fisher, then mistress of Westover, he went outside to say hello. There was no one there. Then, he thought that if he had seen a woman at eye level, since his kitchen is raised, she would have had to be at least 10 feet tall!

But of all who have claimed sightings of Evelyn, no one yet has offered a reasonable explanation as to why her restless

Miss Evelyn Byrd

spirit would want to periodically return to a place which apparently caused her so much unhappiness in life. Some people speculate that ghosts return to the world of the living to carry out some "unfinished business." Could it possibly be that Evelyn comes back to "announce" that she has been reunited with her English lover; that she has found in death the bliss she had been denied in life?

*   *   *   *

Evelyn's spirit is not the only one to haunt the Byrd family, however. There also, allegedly, is the ghost of Elizabeth

Carter Byrd, who at age 16 married Evelyn's brother, William Byrd III in 1748, 11 years after Evelyn's death. And so it was either at Westover or at another Byrd home at "Belvidere," historians are in some disagreement as to which, that tragedy struck once again.

Elizabeth's life with William Byrd III was not happy. Her mother in law, Moriah Taylor, despised her and treated her with abrasiveness and disdain. Elizabeth bore five children during her 11 years of marriage and "grieved bitterly" when two of her boys were sent to England for schooling. She never was to see them again.

William Byrd III, like his father, was a prominent Virginian, but he had two human failings: he gambled to excess, often losing large sums, and he was a womanizer. Apparently out of spite, Moriah Taylor told Elizabeth one day that if she looked in the large chest-on-chest in the upstairs bedroom she would find evidence of her husband's illicit affairs in the form of love letters.

Unable to curb her curiosity, and suspecting the worst, Elizabeth approached the huge chest, but could not reach the top drawer. So she pulled out some lower drawers and stepped up on them. Her screams were clearly heard throughout the house as the chest toppled forward on her. By the time others reached her she was dead; crushed to death.

Ever since that day servants have told of hearing high pitched calls for help coming from that bedroom. One was James Adkins, who served as a butler to Mrs. Ramsey in the early 1900s. He said many times he heard a woman calling from over the bannister on the third floor. And each time he went upstairs there was no one there. "It's like you were being called to do something, but there was no one in the house," he said.

There are two theories as to the origin of the pleas for help. One is that it is Elizabeth, begging for aid, the heavy chest pinning her still to the floor. But others believe that the voice is that of Moriah Taylor's. For it is said that in life she never forgave herself for inciting her daughter-in-law to take the action which caused her death. So it may be the ghost of Moriah Taylor which comes back seeking the aid of someone to stop the ill-fated Elizabeth from climbing up the chest.

*   *   *   *

And finally there is the curious tale of William Byrd III. Just six months after Elizabeth was buried, he married Mary Willing of Philadelphia, "a woman of great ability." They were very happy for a number of years, but as one historian-author wrote, "love is powerless to alter life's great degree: he who dances must lay the music's price."

Late in December 1776, distraught at having squandered much of his family's fortune, which led to the eventual sale of Westover out of the family, William Byrd III took his own life in a "certain chamber" of the house before the fireplace where he often sat in a favorite armchair.

A century and a half later a guest at the plantation, enthralled with the ghostly legends, spent the night in the same chamber. He was standing in the room gazing at the door just as the grandfather clock struck 12 times. Midnight. Then, he saw the door opening. Just at that precise moment an "awful crash" resounded through the house.

The door opened slowly, deliberately, and a "shadowy, icy presence seemed to glide past the great bedstead and then to the chintz covered chair. Its vapory unreality filled not only the chair, but the room, and turned the atmosphere into the chill of death."

It was, the excited visitor said the next morning, the spectral reappearance of the great house's former master. He knew, because the apparition matched perfectly the features and dress of the portrait of William Byrd III which hangs at Westover!

About the Author

L. B. Taylor, Jr. — a Scorpio — is a native Virginian. He was born in Lynchburg and has a BS degree in Journalism from Florida State University. He wrote about America's space programs for 16 years, for NASA and aerospace contractors, before moving to Williamsburg, Virginia, in 1974, as public affairs director for BASF Corporation. He retired in 1993. Taylor is the author of more than 300 national magazine articles and 30 nonfiction books. His research for the book "Haunted Houses," published by Simon and Schuster in 1983, stimulated his interest in area psychic phenomena and led to the publication of five regional Virginia ghost books preceding "The Ghosts of Virginia."